Joy World

"TEACH ME YOUR WAYS, O LORD,
THAT I MAY LIVE ACCORDING
TO YOUR TRUTH!"

Psalm 86:11

_____

- -

_____

HOW TO USE THIS BOOK

Set aside time each day to discover...study... enjoy... learn... the Christmas story. You can study/write each verse in one day, or take a couple days to complete the "lesson."

First, look up the Scripture passage in your Bible.

 **READ** Matthew 1:18-25

 **QUICK TIPS** Read the entire passage listed with your child, even though they are only copying a portion of it. The traceable verse is from the NLT version of the Bible.

 **QUICK TIPS** Make sure you help your child understand the meaning of the words in the verse (Do you know what "sin" means? It means to offend God or to wander away from Him.)

Trace the letters in the Bible verse.

TRACE

WRITE

TRACE & WRITE

"She will have a son, and

"She will _____

you are to name him _____

_____

Jesus, for he will save his _____

_____

people from their sins." _____

_____

Write the verse on your own.

 **QUICK TIPS** Your child can either trace the entire verse at once, and then write it on their own; or trace the words on one line, write it on the following line, trace the next line, write it on the following, etc.

 **QUICK TIPS** If writing the entire verse is too difficult for your child, pick out a couple words for them to write instead.

Draw a picture to illustrate the Bible verses

DRAW

His name is Jesus, & he will save us from our sin!

QUICK TIPS When you illustrate the verse, it helps you take the time to understand what the passage means.

Sing the words of the Scripture to the tune of the song listed. When we sing something, it helps us remember! By putting the verse to song (and adding some actions), memorization will be fun and easy.

SING

And she will have	(Away in a manger)
A so..n	(No crib for a bed)
And you are to name	(The little Lord Jesus)
Him Je..sus	(Laid down His sweet head)
For he will save	(The stars in the bright sky)
His people	(Looked down where He lay)
From their sins	(The little Lord Jesus)
From their sins	(Asleep on the hay)

QUICK TIPS It helps if you hum the tune to the song first to get the tempo and tune. Then sing the words in a way that fits. Sometimes you need to "draw out" the words to fit the tempo of the song.

QUICK TIPS Drawing and singing helps kids enjoy learning! Let this be a time where you participate with them in being creative and moving around.

John 3:16-17

"For this is how God

loved the world:

He gave his one and

only Son...."

 Draw a picture to illustrate the Bible verses.

 "For this is how God loved the world: He gave his one and only Son...." John 3:16

Sing the verse to the tune of "Jingle Bells".

This is how	(Jingle bells)
Go..d	(jingle bells)
lo..ved the world	(jingle all the way)
He...	(Oh what fun)
Ga..ve	(it is to ride)
His one and only Son!	(in a one horse open sleigh!)

John 1:1-14

"So the Word became

human and made his

home among us."

 Draw a picture to illustrate the Bible verses.

 "So the Word became human and made his home among us." John 1:14 **Sing the verse to the tune of "We Wish You A Merry Christmas"**

So the Word became human   (We wish you a Merry Christmas)
And made his home among us (We wish you a Merry Christmas)
So the Word became human   (We wish you a Merry Christmas)
John 1:14   (And a Happy New Year)

TRACE & WRITE

"Because God's children

are human beings...

the Son also became

flesh and blood."

 Draw a picture to illustrate the Bible verses.

 "Because God's children are human beings--made of flesh and blood--the Son also became flesh and blood." Hebrews 2:14 **Sing the verse to the tune of "Let it Snow."**

Because God's children are human

    (Oh, the weather outside is frightful)

Made of flesh and blood

    (But the fire is so delightful)

So the Son also became

    (Since we've no place to go)

Flesh and blood, flesh and blood, flesh and blood

    (Let it snow, let it snow, let it snow)

Luke 1:26-33

"Don't be afraid, Mary,"

the angel told her,

"for you have found

favor with God!"

 Draw a picture to illustrate the Bible verses.

 "Don't be afraid, Mary," the angel told her, "for you have found favor with God!" Luke 1:30

Sing the verse to the tune of "Frosty the Snowman."

Don't be afraid	(Frosty the snowman)
The angel told Mary	(Was a jolly happy soul)
For you have found	(With a corn cob pipe)
favor	(and a button nose)
wi..th God!	(And two eyes made out of coal)

TRACE & WRITE

"So the baby to be

born will be holy, and

he will be called the

Son of God."

DRAW Draw a picture to illustrate the Bible verses.

SING "So the baby to be born will be holy, and he will be called the Son of God." Luke 1:35

Sing the verse to the tune of "Joy to the World."

So the baby   (Joy to the world)

To be born   (the Lord is come)

Will be holy   (Let Earth receive her King)

And he will be   (Let every heart)

ca...lled   (prepare Him room)

The Son of God   (And Heaven and nature sing)

The Son of God   (And Heaven and nature sing)

And he will be called the Son of God

     (And Heaven, and Heaven, and nature sing)

TRACE & WRITE

"You are blessed

because you believed

that the Lord would do

what he said."

 Draw a picture to illustrate the Bible verses.

 "You are blessed because you believed that the Lord would do what he said." Luke 1:45

Sing the verse to the tune of "Rudolph the Red-Nosed Reindeer"

You are blessed	(Rudolph the Red-Nosed Reindeer)
Because you believed	(Had a very shiny nose)
That the Lord would	(And if you ever saw it)
Do what he said	(You would even say it glows)
You are blessed	(All of the other reindeer)
Because you believed	(Used to laugh and call him names)
That the Lord would	(They never let poor Rudolph)
Do what he said!	(Join in any reindeer games)

"Oh, how my soul

praises the Lord.

How my spirit rejoices

in God my Savior!"

Draw a picture to illustrate the Bible verses.

"Oh, how my soul praises the Lord. How my spirit rejoices in God my Savior!" Luke 1:46

Sing the verse to the tune of "Go Tell it on the Mountain."

Oh, how my soul	(Go, tell it on the mountain)
Praises the Lo...rd	(Over the hills and everywhere)
How my spirit rejoices	(Go, tell it on the mountain)
In God my Savior!	(That Jesus Christ is born)

TRACE & WRITE

"She will have a son, and

you are to name him

Jesus, for he will save his

people from their sins."

DRAW Draw a picture to illustrate the Bible verses.

SING "She will have a son, and you are to name him Jesus, for he will save his people from their sins." Matt. 1:21
Sing the verse to the tune of "Away in a Manger."

And she will have	(Away in a manger)
A so..n	(No crib for a bed)
And you are to name	(The little Lord Jesus)
Him Je..sus	(Laid down His sweet head)
For he will save	(The stars in the bright sky)
His people	(Looked down where He lay)
From their sins	(The little Lord Jesus)
From their sins	(Asleep on the hay)

Luke 2:1-7

"She wrapped him snugly

in strips of cloth and

laid him in a manger..."

 **Draw a picture to illustrate the Bible verses.**

 "She wrapped him snugly in strips of cloth and laid him in a manger...." Luke 2:7

Sing the verse to the tune of "We Wish You A Merry Christmas."

She wrapped him all snugly   (We wish you a Merry Christmas)

In strips o..f clo..th   (We wish you a Merry Christmas)

And laid him in a manger   (We wish you a Merry Christmas)

Luke 2:7   (And a Happy New Year)

Luke 2:8-20

"Don't be afraid...I I

I bring you good news

that will bring great joy

to all people."

 Draw a picture to illustrate the Bible verses.

 "Don't be afraid!" he said. "I bring you good news that will bring great joy to all people." Luke 2:10

Sing the verse to the tune of "Jesus Loves Me".

Don't be afraid	(Jesus loves me)
He said	(this I know)
I bring you good news	(for the Bible tells me so)
That will bring great joy	(little ones to him belong)
To all people.	(they are weak but he is strong)
I bring you good news!	(Yes, Jesus loves me)
I bring you good news!	(Yes, Jesus loves me)
I bring you good news!	(Yes, Jesus loves me)
Great joy to all people!	(The Bible tells me so)

Matthew 2:1-12

"Where is the newborn

king of the Jews? We

saw his star as it rose..."

 **DRAW** Draw a picture to illustrate the Bible verses.

 **SING** "Where is the newborn king of the Jews? We saw his star as it rose, and we have come to worship him." Matt. 2:2

Sing the verse to the tune of "Where is Thumbkin".

Where is the	(Where is thumbkin)
Newborn King	(Where is thumbkin?)
Of the Jews	(Here I am)
Of the Jews	(Here I am)
We saw his star	(How are you this morning?)
As it rose	(Very well, I thank you)
We have come	(Run away)
To worship him	(Run away)

TRACE & WRITE

"Wonderful Counselor,

Mighty God,

Everlasting Father,

Prince of Peace."

 Draw a picture to illustrate the Bible verses.

 "And he will be called: Wonderful Counselor, Mighty God, Everlasting Father, Prince of Peace." Isaiah 9:6

Sing the verse to the tune of "Rudolph the Red-Nose Reindeer

Wonderful Counselor (Rudolph the Red-Nosed Reindeer)
Mighty God   (Had a very shiny nose)
Everlasting Father   (And if you ever saw it)
Prince of Peace   (You would even say it glows)

If you need tools to help your children grow in
their walk with the Lord, use this QR Code to go to

DIGGINGINTOGOD.COM